365 Days
of
Writing Nonfiction

By Charlotte Hopkins

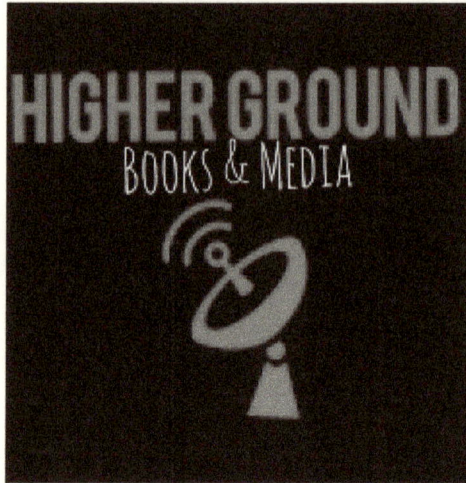

Unless otherwise noted, all Scripture quotations are from the Holy Bible, New King James Version. Copyright © 1979, 1980, 1982, 1995.

Higher Ground Books & Media
Springfield, Ohio.
http://highergroundbooksandmedia.com

Printed in the United States of America 2019

365 Days
of
Writing Nonfiction

By Charlotte Hopkins

INTRODUCTION

Writer's block can be one of the largest hurdles to overcome. So, get your pen and paper out and get a jump ahead by following this timeline of thought provoking writing ideas. Creative writing prompts to fill the next 365 days ahead will help to polish your writing and possibly generate your next best seller!

Begin a journey of new writing, whether it is January 1st or the end of summer. Battling the dreadful writer's block has never been so easy. Remember, one great idea can lead to another; setting off a domino effect of successful writing.

<u>JANUARY</u>:

January 1: Write at least one article a day. At the end of the year you will have 365 articles to work with!

January 2: Start the year with an empty jar and fill it with notes of good things that happen, then on New Year's Eve, empty it and see what awesome stuff happened that year!

January 3: Create an "All About Me" journal. You can include photos, memories and special messages!

January 4: Make a Q&A piece on any subject holiday trivia.

January 5: Celebrate National Bird Day by writing an article on the wide variety of birds or focus on a favorite one!

January 6: Choose a location or "spot" that is special to you. What do you like about it? How did you find it? What was your first visit like?

January 7: Create a profile piece of your favorite biker friend!

January 8: "Who the hell wants to hear actors talk?" Harry Warner, Warner Brothers, 1927, in response to the beginning of talking pictures. Map out a Timeline of Movie History – include movie trivia! End it with a list of your 10 favorite movies.

January 9: Make a how-to guide to creating a fun baby shower – games and decorations!

January 10: For "Houseplant Appreciation Day," write about all the ways to create beautiful houseplants and even a home garden.

January 11: Write about how to start and run a book club!

January 12: What was one of the best meals you ever had? Write about the company, the day, and why it was your favorite meal.

January 13: Write a story around a medical miracle – your own or someone else's. Even an encouraging piece about someone rescuing another person.

January 14: Write about a time that you were sick.

January 15: Write about someone who was a hero to you.

January 16: Write about your old bedroom, from any time period, and the feelings that it brings back for you.

January 17: Make a list of stress busters!

January 18: What thoughts does the word "blue" bring on for you?

January 19: Write about a time when you learned who your true friends are.

January 20: It is Penguin Awareness Day! Spend the day at the Aviary, learning about penguins (some will even let you feed them!). Also visit the home of the penguins at the Pittsburgh Zoo. Write an article on everything you learned.

January 21: Today is Martin Luther King Jr. Day! He is famous for his "I Have a Dream Speech. Have lunch with a friend, and the two of you discuss your own dream. Write out the plans you need to achieve that dream. Then start pursuing it! Good Luck!!

January 22: Write 100 activities to do outside in the snow.

January 23: Write about everything that you enjoy about science!

January 24: It is "Compliment Day!" Go through each of your facebook friends and post a compliment on their wall!

January 25: Write about your favorite hobby as if you were teaching someone else.

January 26: Have you ever felt like you witnessed a miracle? Do you believe in miracles?

January 27: Write about a pet that you loved and cared for as a favor for a friend.

January 28: Write 100 Lessons Life Taught Me – Advice for the Next Generation

January 29: If an emergency caused you to evacuate your home and you could only bring 10 things with you, what would they be and why?

January 30: What are all the things you can do when the electricity goes out.

January 31: Think of a struggle that you overcame. Write an article that will help others going through that same circumstance.

FEBRUARY:

February 1: For Black History Month, write a timeline of African American History.

February 2: Write about the history of Groundhog's Day. Start with the German immigrants and the reporter who started the fable of Punxsutawney Phil.

February 3: Today is "The day the music died." It marks the death of Buddy Holly, Richie Valens and the Big Bopper in a plane crash in 1959. Write a musical history piece of other musicians who died at either a young age or at the start of their career.

February 4: What is everything that you would teach students today, that isn't taught in schools anymore?

February 5: For American Heart Month, write about the ways to living a healthier lifestyle – physically and mentally?

February 6: Do you remember the coldest that you have ever been? Describe what was happening.

February 7: The Beatles arrived in America on February 7, 1963. What are the changes that the Beatles brought to the music world? Describe the characteristics of the Beatles and all the people they influenced.

February 8: Write a survival guide piece on weather disasters.

February 9: What is your favorite event in American history?

February 10: Make homemade Valentine cards for the troops in Iraq. Contact either "Soldier's Angels" or Adopt-a-Platoon to get an address on where to send the cards.

February 11: "If I fall asleep with a pen in my hand, don't remove it - I might be writing in my dreams," is a quote by blogger Danzae Pace. Write about the last dream that you can remember. Also write about dreams that you had in the past that you still remember and why!

February 12: Abraham Lincoln had a hard life. What was it like?

February 13: During "Creative Romance Month," write about your first crush....and your first love!

February 14: Make a list of all the ways to say "I love you!"

February 15: What was your first job? What mistakes did you make? What was memorable about it?

February 16: The internet can be the best friend of a home business owner. the websites Kickstarter and Indiegogo are resources to raise the money needed to start a business. The websites facebook, Etsey, and Pinterest can be used to promote your business. Write about how these websites together can help a person start and run a home/small business.

February 17: For "Random Acts of Kindness Day," write 365 acts of kindness and start from today; doing one every day. And this time next year...make another list. You can re-add your favorites and some new ones as well!

February 18: Celebrate President's day with a history of the US Presidents. Start with George Washington and how he declined the the offer to be king of the United States, opting instead to be president and create a democracy instead of a monarchy. How have the ideals of the presidency changed. Have their been presidents who were less than honorable to the office of presidency?

February 19: Write a history of names - unique, funny, creative and inspirational names through history. How did your parents choose your name? Does it hold a significant meaning to you? Has your name ever helped or hurt you? What nicknames have you been branded with? If you could change your name to anything, what would it be, and why?

February 20: Write about a day that changed your life!

February 21: What is your favorite season? List all the reasons why it is your favorite.

February 22: Today is George Washington's birthday! One of the favorite stories of George Washington was that he once chopped down a cherry tree and when his father asked him if he did it, he said - "I can not tell a lie, yes, I chopped down the cherry tree. Write a how-to article around your favorite cherry recipes – pie, cookies, smoothie and even a jubilee.

February 23: Pick a sport that you are curious about, but unfamiliar with, and write the history behind it, Do your research and go back to the days it was first created. Whose idea was it? Who are some of the more outstanding athletes in that sport?

February 24: Write an encouraging piece on all the steps a person can take to find a job.

February 25: Write a historical piece about the town that you live in now.

February 26: Write a biography piece about a person who makes a difference in their community.

February 27: Write about something that you collect or always wanted to start collecting. Describe why you want to collect these things, the history behind your collection, and the items themselves.

February 28: What is your most prized possession? What is the history behind it and why is it important to you?

MARCH:

March 1: Write fun poems that teach children math and science facts.

March 2: This is "Old Stuff Day!" Visit an antique store and write about the historical items that you find there. Write about how other objects got their start. For example:

*Beads were first made in Tibet and had human bone in them.

*Chewing Gum was first made in sticks in 1872 and Blackjack was the first of it"s kind!

*Flashlights earned their name because when they were introduced, the bulbs and batteries were not made well and would only stay on for a few seconds at a time.

March 3: What was the worst relationship you ever had and why you stayed? What did it teach you about relationships?

March 4: During National Woman's History Month, write about a woman who made a difference in her community.

March 5: For National Craft Month, write a how-to piece around your favorite craft projects. It can be anything from decorating tote bags, magnets, or even jars of trail mix and soup ingredients.

March 6: What are some things that were invented accidentally?

March 7: What are your best tips for staying safe on the road? What are some items that you think everyone should carry – and why?

March 8: Write a parenting article with your best advice on communication and discipline.

March 9: This is "Music in our Schools Month," practice writing songs – for teens and adults or children! You may discover a writing style that you are pretty good at!

March 10: Write about a wish that came true, just not the way you expected it to.

March 11: Write a how-to article on being the perfect party host. And how to play host to out-of-town friends.

March 12: It was said that, "Opportunities are never missed: Someone will take the ones you miss." Write about an opportunity that you were afraid to take.

March 13: What is the best advice you would give someone on dealing with tough in-laws.

March 14: What was your most rewarding moment?

March 15: For "Potato Chip Day" write about the history of the flavors that came and went. What would it be like to work in the potato chip factory as a flavor scientist or even a crunch tester?

March 16: What was the most difficult decision that you ever had to make?

March 17: Happy St. Patrick's Day! What better way to celebrate than writing about the history of the Irish. Include the discrimination they faced when they first came to America.

March 18: What were your favorite toys as a child. Do they reflect who you are today?

March 19: If you could start your own magazine on any subject – what would it be about? Who would advertise in it? Who would the magazine be geared towards?

March 20: For "Proposal Day," write all the creative ways to propose to someone!

March 21: Tell the history of the cowboys!

March 22: Write about unusual careers of yesterday and today.

March 23: For National Peanut Month, write about all the creative uses for peanut butter – including the fun smoothies and treats!

March 24: Do you believe in God? How did you come to that decision?

March 25: What are all the ways that schools can put an end to bullying?

March 26: Write about the history of art/photography and the different styles. Do a focus piece on your favorite artist/photographer.

March 27: Write about different types of fund raisers for schools/organizations.

March 28: Write an information piece about your favorite animal! Include movies that your favorite animal played a role.

March 29: It is National Mom and Pop Business Owners Day! Talk to a small business owner about how they got started. Write about the ups and downs of owning a business. Write about the difficulties and awards that await them.

March 30: What are your favorite fads that you would like to see come back. What are some of the more odd fads that you are happy to see go!

March 31: Write a story about your best Easter! Now write about your worst Easter!

APRIL

April 1: Write about a joke that was played on you and all of the jokes that you would play on people – if you could get away with it!

April 2: For Autism Awareness Day, write an informative piece to educate the public on autism. How can people understand what happens to children and adults affected by autism. What are some of the possible causes? How have doctors and parents thrived by teaming together to fight autism?

April 3: The first sundae was made on April 3, 1892 by John Scott, a Unitarian church minister, and Chester Platt, owner of Platt and Colt pharmacy. The flavors were Cherry Sunday, Strawberry Sunday and Chocolate Sunday. They were made with ice cream, cherry syrup and candied cherries. The name was changed to "sundae" 2 years later. Write a fun recipe book on all the creative ways to make sundaes.

April 4: Write an opinion piece about gay marriage.

April 5: Write about all the ways to create a dream wedding on a shoestring budget!

April 6: April Showers, Bring May Flowers! Learn all the interesting facts about the weather, including natural disasters in history. Include the "Dust Bowl" of the mid-west.

April 7: "Keep America Beautiful" month, write 101 things that can be recycled and how – be creative!

April 8: Two states have made it legal to smoke marijuana. What is your opinion of this? What are the pros and cons of marijuana usage?

April 9: What is everything that you would take on a road trip with your friends....or your family. Where would you stop along the way. Write about destinations in America that you always wanted to see – and why.

April 10: Write about a feud that you had with a friend.

April 11: Write about a time that you tried to cook and nothing worked out.

April 12: Write about the history of food. Or narrow it down to cereal, candy or snacks!

April 13: It is National Poetry Month! Write poems of your favorite genre and send them out to greeting card companies!

April 14: It was on April 24, 1912 that the Titanic struck an iceberg and sank, killing more than 1500 people on board. Write about the events of that night, as well as, other tragedies at sea.

April 15: Write a step-by-step guide to building a mancave!

April 16: Write about an experience you had with extreme weather.

April 17: Write about all the ways people can strengthen their communication skills.

April 18: For Newspaper's Columnists Day, start a newsletter at your place of employment or church. You can even start a family newsletter!

April 19: Write an article for parents on a child health issue, such as, chicken pox, allergies, teething, or how to stock a homemade first aid kit.

April 20: Write all of the good and bad points about facebook.

April 21: Visit the library and choose a random nonfiction book from the shelf. Write the title of chapter 4 from the index and write an article from that.

April 22: What is your pet peeve and why?

April 23: Write a list of 100 things you can do inside on a rainy day.

April 24: In honor of "International Guitar Month" write about guitarists through history from Buddy Holly and George Harrison to Eddie Van Halen, and Jimmy Hendrix.

April 25: Write about the Amish life, their history and beliefs!

April 26: Write about everything that you enjoy about animals!

April 27: Today is "Tell a Story Day!" Write about the history of books. The first self help books. Books that made a difference. Self published books, like, The Joy of Cooking, and What to Expect when You're Expecting, that went on to be best sellers! Include all of the books that you think children and teens should read. Write all of the books that you think adults should even read. Here are some fun book facts:

*Agatha Christie's books have been translated into 44 languages – the most of any author!

*Hans Christian Anderson wrote 168 fairy tales.

*Every 40 seconds, somewhere in the world, a child starts reading a Harry Potter book.

April 28: For International Astronomy Day, choose an astronaut and write a story about them.

April 29: Write an "ABC Guide," using each letter of the alphabet. It can be for children, with such as, baseball facts or animal facts. Or it can be an easy read for busy parents with subjects like cooking, decorating or homeschooling children. For example:

An A-Z Guide to Homeschooling:

*Amerca is referred to as a "melting pot" because people from countries around the world came to this country to start a new life, a new nation – a new world! Emphasize the different nationalities by listing 10 facts of each nation. the final list can be dedicated to America as a whole!

*Books can be written on virtually any subject! Spend the day at the library searching out 10 of the oddest but most interesting books and create lessons around them!

*Cows drink a bathtub full of water and eat 40 pounds of food a day. What are other facts that you can learn about life on a farm?

April 30: Today is National Honesty Day! Write about everything that you have ever held inside. Your hopes, fears, goals, and wishes!

MAY

May 1: Did you know that Albert Einstein never wore socks and that Thomas Wolfe wrote on sheets of yellow paper with pencil stubs he kept in a coffee can!?! What are some your writing niches? Write about the habits of other writers as well. What are some of the common everyday habits of writers as a whole? These can be things, such as, keeping pen and paper next to the bed, coming up with story ideas at the strangest places, and checking baby name websites for unique character names.

May 2: Practice writing limericks!

May 3: Write about the escalation of crime and all the ways that people can stay safe today.

May 4: This is International Firefighter Day! Write about the heroic acts of firefighters. Include firefighters who dies in the line of duty!

May 5: Write trivia facts about Irish history.

May 6: Who was your favorite teacher and why? What are all the things you would teach students today.

May 7: Now write about a teacher who gave you a difficult time.

May 8: What were some of your favorite places to visit when you were a child?

May 9: What are all the ways to have a fun and profitable yard sale?

May 10: In honor of National Photograph Month, visit your favorite park or take a walk through your community, taking dozens of photographs along the way. Turn it into a photo-journal about the day.

May 11: For Twilight Zone Day, write about the most bizarre thing that ever happened to you or something that strange that you witnessed.

May 12: Write a Mother's Day piece about women who made a difference in the lives of children.

May 13: Write a piece all about boats. Include the history of boating, the different styles of boats and all of the uses of boats – from recreation, to travel, to a means of employment! Boats can include pontoon boats, ships, cruise lines, and even kayaks!

May 14: This is Police Week, write a story about the police and their heroic acts that don't make the evening news.

May 15: The expression, "Garbage in, Garbage out," was originated by computer programmers. Write about a time in your life when you had to make the desion to rid your life of every negative aspect and every negative person that was holding you down.

May 16: What are your earliest memories of visiting an amusement park?

May 17: Tell the story behind the practice of forensics.

May 18: On Armed Forces Day write letters of thanks and encouragement and send them to military troop troops in Iraq and Afghanistan,

May 19: Write about someone you loved that has passed away. What are some things that you can do to honor their memory?

May 20: For Emergency Medical Services Week, write about the day in the life of a paramedic.

May 21: For National Memo Day, invest in Post-It Notes and leave messages all over for friends, family, neighbors, and co-workers.

May 22: Write about HOMES – the different types of home....and what makes a home!

May 23: Write about planning an event – anything from an anniversary to a grand opening of sorts.

May 24: Interview a senior citizen and write about their stories.

May 25: What was the worst experience you had in a restaurant?

May 26: Memorial Day, is celebrated the last Monday of each May. On this day we honor the men and women who died while serving in the military. Visit a military museum and write about the lives of the soldiers at war – and the great sacrifices they made to defend our freedom.

May 27: Dracula was published on May 27, 1897 by Anne Rice. Write about the history of vampires.

May 28: What is your biggest fear and how can you overcome it?

May 29: Write about internet safety – for children, teens, and adults!

May 30: If you could go back and give your younger self advice, what would it be?

May 31: What are all the beliefs of time travel? Do you agree? Why or Why Not?

JUNE

June 1: A favorite summer activity is horseback riding. Write about the sport of horseback riding – how to do it safely, what you should carry with you, and everything you should know about horses.

June 2: For Aquarium Month, write a fun piece about everything that can be found in the waters, such as, fish, dolphin, an octopus, jellyfish, seaweed, an old tire and even a wrecked boat!

June 3: "If I had thought about it, I wouldn't have done the experiment. The literature was full of examples that said you can't do this." - Spencer Silver, the creator of Post-It Notes. Write about a time when people told you that you could not achieve a goal and you proved them wrong.

June 4: Write about the future of home businesses. Include an inspirational piece about a successful home business owner. What inspired them and what were some of their growing pains along the way. What are the good and bad aspects of working from home?

June 5: US President Ronald Reagan died from Alzheimer's on June 5, 2004. Write about Alzheimer's disease. What do scientists believe is at the root of the disease? What are some of the steps they have taken to find a cure?

June 6: Now today write a step-by-step guide on starting and running a home business. Begin with how to choose the right business and go from there.

June 7: What would be your dream job/jobs (You can have more than one!) How would your day start and end?

June 8: For Best Friends Day, write about your best friend. How did you meet? What are the good and bad traits of your friend? What are the ups and downs that you and your friend have been through?

June 9: Write 101 tips for gardeners.

June 10: Write an inspirational pieces for everyone graduating from college – include young adults who are just starting in the world and older adults who went back to learn a new trade!

June 11: Write about allergies – both seasonal allergies and food allergies. What are some of the symptoms and remedies for allergies.

June 12: Celebrate Rose Month by writing about the first time that someone gave you flowers. Or a time when you gave someone else flowers.

June 13: Write about your addictions – from coffee to cigarettes.

June 14: To celebrate Flag Day, write a story about the rich heritage of the American flag and what it means to you.

June 15: Write about your time away at summer camp. If you did not go to camp, create a story of what you think it would be like.

June 16: Write a Father's Day piece about men who made a difference in the lives of children.

June 17: Write an historical piece about amphibians, from turtles and snakes, all the way back to the days of the dinosaurs.

June 18: Write about the history of words, from the days that a pillow case was called a slip cover – to the days of "groovy" and "gag me with a spoon" - to regional dialects, such as California, lingo, southern talk, and even "Pittsburghese!"

June 19: Write a story of the history of Kennywood (or your local amusement park), including, how the park got it's start, snacks, rides, activities, and tragedies.

June 20: Write a first person account about an accident that you were in – be it a car accident, bike accident, or a bad fall.

June 21: Write a "Best of...." article, such as, the best hot dog stands, best parks, best libraries, best museums, etc.

June 22: Write a "Psychology Piece" about any type of human behavior.

June 23: If you were giving someone a tour of your community, what would you show them?

June 24: Write about astrology; the different signs, their meanings and stories behind them.

June 25: Think about a time that you got lost! Where were you going? Who helped you find your way back?

June 26: Write about everything that new parents will need for their baby's nursery. Include decorating tips!

June 27: Write about the history of transportation – everything from wagons and trains – to trucks and roller skating. What could be other forms of transportation in the future?

Did you know that it wasn't until 1949 that cars were made to start by turning a key only?

June 28: Write about some of the best medical breakthroughs, from the tongue depressor to the cure for small pox!

June 29: Write about the different types of alternative healing, such as, reflexology, acupuncture, and Coin Rubbing.

June 30: Write a biography about someone in history that you greatly admire!

JULY

July 1: Write a Q&A piece on American history.

July 2: For World UFO Day, write about your opinion on whether there is life on other planets. Do you believe that aliens have visited us?

July 3: Though we are the 50 United States, each state has it"s own characteristics. Write about what they are.

July 4: Happy 4th of July!! This is the birthday of the United States, referred to as "Independence Day," as we won our independence from England. Write about American Values from then and now,

July 5: Write the plot for a movie where you and your friends are the characters. Include co-workers, neighbors and the people who drive you crazy and aggravate you, as well!

July 6: Write trivia facts about the forefathers in our country.

July 7: What are all of the ways that writers can earn money at their craft?

July 8: Ernest Hemingway once said: *I love sleep. My life has the tendency to fall apart when I'm awake, you know?*

Write about "sleep" and everything we know and wonder about it. This can include, sleep patterns, nightmares, levels of sleep and even dreams.

July 9: Write about trying to satisfy a picky eater and the ways to "trick" them into trying new foods?

July 10: Write an article for parents on how to safety proof their home.

July 11: Write a survival guide for single parents!

July 12: Debbie Fields, embarrassed by the host of a party for mispronouncing a word, was inspired to launch her own business, just to show this rude man up. In 1977, as a young mother with no business experience, Mrs. Fields opened her first cookie store. Write about a time when someone's negative behavior, angered you to do something to spite him.

July 13: Celebrate "Embrace Your Geekness Day," by writing a step-by-step guide to building a website. What are the popular websites online today?

July 14: Write about why music is important to you. Which songs hold a special meaning to you?

July 15: Write about divorce. Have you experienced divorce? Have you seen others go through this?

July 16: Write about everything that you know and enjoy about your favorite sport!

July 17: Write about a day when you missed the bus. Did your plans for that day change for the better?

July 18: In 1969, Hurricane Camille went through the state of Virginia. Clyde and Ginger Harvey owned apple orchards that were destroyed by Camille. Several years later, they found an apple tree growing from a seed that was washed in from the storm. The new apple was named Ginger Gold after Mrs. Harvey. Write about something good that came from a tragedy in your life.

July 19: Rearrange or reword a cliche to start an article or story, for example...

"DON'T WORRY, BE HAPPY" to "DON'T WORRY, BE YOURSELF"

"THE CALM BEFOR ETHE STORM" to "IS THIS THE CALM BEFORE THE STORM?"

"EVERY DOG HAS IT'S TODAY" to "EVERY DOG HAS IT'S DAY~AND TODAY I WAS THE DOG"

"IN SEVENTH HEAVEN" to "ON CLOUD NINE IN SEVENTH HEAVEN"

"A DIAMOND IN THE ROUGH" to "A DIAMOND IN THE ROUGH – THE TEEN YEARS!"

July 20: For National Hot Dog Month, write about all the creative ways to make hot dogs! Talk to a hot dog vendor and find out what his day is like. Write about restaurants across the country that specialize in hot dogs!!

July 21: Write about your most memorable summer. What were the good and bad that happened that summer? What is it about that summer that stands out the most?

July 22: If you could visit another country what would it be and why?

July 23: Write all of the ways that you feel technology has helped or hurt society.

July 24: For Amelia Earhart Day, write about women who became a credit to their profession – regardless of the status of the occupation.

July 25: Write about a time that you were raging with jealousy.

July 26: Besides hot dogs and pretzels, what are 50 things that you would like to see street vendors sell?

July 27: What is the worst experience you had with a prescription medicine or an over-the-counter drug?

July 28: Write about camping – what to take and tips for setting up a camp site. Include advice on activities and safety precautions. Don't forget the S'mores!

July 29: The World War II museum being built in New York, will be the first of it's kind to include the contributions of the Merchant Marines. Write about the history of the Merchant Marines.

July 30: What are some creative excuses to get out of jury duty?

July 31: What was your worst experience with birth control!

AUGUST

August 1: Write a how-to recipe piece about all of the dishes you can cook and create using a slow cooker.

August 2: Write a bucket list – make it as long as you want it!

August 3: John Wayne said, "Courage is being scared to death and saddling up anyway." Write about a time in your life when that describes your situation.

August 4: The first Sunday in August is Friendship Day! Write about the first time you bonded with your best friend.

August 5: Today is "Work Like a Dog Day" but instead of working like a dog – work with the dogs. Volunteer at an animal shelter and write about what it is like for the people and the animals there.

August 6: Write creative study habits and test taking tips for high school students.

August 7: This is National Lighthouse Day! Write about the history of lighthouses. What was their significant use? Highlight some of the more unique and well-known lighthouses.

August 8: Do you believe in reincarnation? Why or why not?

August 9: It is Book Lover's Day! Start an idea journal. Make a list of book titles that you have been working on or would want to write someday.

August 10: Write an advice piece on moving – include packing tips, suggestions on settling into your new home, how to keep in touch with old friends, and making an easy transition for you and your family.

August 11: Write about all the wedding trends in America and how they got their start. Also write about the wedding trends of other nationalities.

August 12: Write about a secret crush that you had when you were younger (or still have today)!

August 13: Write about your favorite conspiracy theories – include all of the beliefs and opinions behind it.

August 14: Write about why children have nightmares. How can parents can help curb them and help children get over fears that stem from their bad dreams. What are some creative tricks that parents use? For example, I gave my daughter a glass egg (it was clear) and I told her that it trapped bad dreams so that she could only have good dreams. It worked!

August 15: Write about all of the ways that we can support and encourage the troops!

August 16: On August 16, 1996, a group of children in India claimed that they were attacked by a werewolf and it killed the youngest child in their group. When did people start believing in werewolves? Write about the history of werewolves. Turn your writing into a Fact vs Myth piece.

August 17: Write a trivia piece on the planets, the sun, the moon – the whole galaxy!

August 18: Write an article for high schoolers making the transfer to college. What can you teach them about life at school (social issues, educational and study habits, safety issues)? Write about what steps they can take now to prepare for their careers.

August 19: Celebrate Aviation Day by spending the afternoon watching the airplanes depart and land at the airport. Write about everything that you saw that day!

August 20: Write a list of home remedies. Here are a few to get you started:

*Yogurt is used to cure bad breath.

*The syrup from a can of fruit cocktail can help stop nausea and vomiting. Take 2 tablespoons every 15 minutes.

August 21: For Zombie Awareness Day, write all of the things that zombie enthusiasts recommend for survival during a zombie apocalypse? What is the history and the beliefs of zombies?

August 22: Make an advice piece for parents who are traveling with their children – include long car rides, plane trips, train rides, and more!

August 23: Write about a time that you or a friend had to stay in the hospital.

August 24: Write a piece for car buyers. What are all of the things people should look for when buying a used car?

August 25: Write about a nonprofit group in your area. What are all the ways, the community can help them?

August 26: Write about a friendship that began – and grew online!

August 27: Write about creative ways to have birthday parties for children – from their first – their 18th birthday.

August 28: Write a Q&A piece on the history of sports.

August 29: Michael Moore invented push pins in 1900. What are some other oh-so-simple inventions that became super successful, such as straws and toothpicks.

August 30: Write about all of the ways that a person can raise their self esteem. Now write one for parents on how they can raise their child:s self esteem.

August 31: For National Trail Mix Day, write a how-to article on all the ways to make Trail Mix and who you would surprise with trail mix gifts today!

SEPTEMBER

September 1: Happy Labor Day! Write about the most difficult, yet most rewarding, experiences that you had on the job. What was the craziest, or the worst, job that you ever had?

September 2: Write about the work of a freelance Art Therapist.

September 3: For Hispanic Heritage Month, write about Hispanics who have made a difference in the world.

September 4: Pick up several newspapers for Newspaper Carrier Day. Write the headlines from various stories and use them as the first sentence in articles that you write about your friends and family.

September 5: For Cheese Pizza Day, order pizzas, bottles of cold pop and invite your friends to have a writing marathon; compare ideas and help each other with writing blocks!

September 6: It is said that you can make more friends in 2 months by becoming interested in other people than you can in 2 years by trying to get people interested in you. So, ask the next person you see what their passion is – and write about it!

September 7: Colorado was the first state to incorporate a Firefighter Appreciation Week which is typically held at the beginning of September. Write about the history of firefighting. Include historical fires, such as the Great Chicago Fire, the Triangle Shirtwaist Factory Fire, and the recent fire in Arizona, that killed the Hotshot Firefighter Crew.

September 8: For Grandparent's Day, write about your good and bad memories with your grandparents. Travel further back and write about your great great grandparents. What do you think they were like?

September 9: For Square Dancing Month, write about the history of the dance. Delve into the subject of all types of dance – ballet, break dancing, line dancing, and more!

September 10: Do you believe in psychics? Why or why not?

September 11: Write about the impact that 9/11 had on you and the world around you. Do you believe that 9/11 should be a national holiday?

September 12: In the tv series, "Quantum Leap," Sam was a scientist who got lost in time from an experiment gone wrong. He spent years leaping through history trying to fix the wrongs in the world. The show ended with Sam never leaping back home. A tv special that all Quantum Leap fans waited for. Write about tv shows that ended oddly.

September 13: Yay for Fortune Cookie Day! Write all of the fortunes that you would give to friends and family. What are all of the fortune telling techniques that people use to tell the future?

September 14: Write about the Philadelphia Experiment. What are your thoughts on the events of that day.

September 15: Write trivia facts around the history of police tv books, movies, and tv shows.

September 16: For Mayflower Day, start tracing your family tree and learn all of your family's interesting stories. It will be fascinating to see how far your family has come. Write about all of your family characteristics along the way – their careers, hobbies, and more!

September 17: Write about how to put together time capsules, hope chests, and other memory makers.

September 18: This is Chicken Month! Visit a local chicken farm and write about the growing craze of people raising their own chickens. Put together a how-to piece on chicken farming.

September 19: Write about a time that you felt life was completely unfair to you.

September 20: If you died tomorrow, how would your obituary read? How would your best friend write your obituary? How would your enemy write your obituary? How would you want your obituary to read? Include everything that you always wished would happen for you.

September 21: Celebrate International Rabbit Day by writing all about bunnies. Write about how rabbits are used for therapeutic uses at Angora Gardens in White Oak, Pennsylvania. How many movies and books featured rabbits?

September 22: Start a story with these words: In five years, will this matter...

September 23: It's Checkers Day! Did you know that Checkers has been played since BC? Write about the history of board games. You will be surprised by what you learn!

September 24: Write about your favorite spot(s) as a teen. Why was it so important?

September 25: For National Comic Book Day, write a comic book of your own. Who are your characters. Write about their every day adventures.

September 26: What are the best movies derived from books. Write about movies that did an injustice to their books. Also, what are some books that should be made into a movie?

September 27: For Native American Day, make a Q&A piece on Native American history.

September 28: For Acknowledge National Good Neighbor Day, write about an adult neighbor that had an impact on you as a child.

September 29: If you could go back in time and witness, change or participate in 5 things what would they be? Why?

September 30: If you were confined to bed rest for a week, what items would you want with you?

OCTOBER

October 1: This is "Get Organized Week!" Make a list of 100 tips to organize your space and time.

October 2: Start a club for writers. The first thing everyone should write about is the day that they knew they wanted to be a writer.

October 3: Write a 20-Line Poem of one of your scariest moments.

October 4: Write down a list of all of your fears. Choose one and write about it.

October 5: In honor of Clergy Appreciation Month, write about your best and your worst experiences in church?

October 6: Write 130 spooky and creative ideas for Halloween parties.

October 7: An Arachnologist studies spiders. Learn about spiders and write a story about it for children and teens.

October 8: Write about the ways to keep your home safe from fire, in honor of Fire Prevention Week. If a fire were to happen, what steps would you take to safely get out. Does your family have a plan?

October 9: For Curious Events Day, write about curiosities, odd facts, outdated laws, and unanswerable questions.

October 10: Write about how your fashion styles have changed through the years. Did you know that until the late 19th century shoes were made to fit either foot? T-shirts were first worn by navy soldiers in the 1930's. Levi Strauss made the first pair of jeans in 1849. Their original purpose was to help gold miners dress more comfortably.

October 11: Write about a real-life murder mystery that was never solved.

October 12: For "Cookbook Launch Day," make a homemade cookbook with your favorite recipes – and even a few new ones that you want to try! Put the pages inside a photo album and make it your Family Holiday cookbook.

October 13: What are some of the craziest superstitions that people believe? Which ones do you believe – and why?

October 14: For Columbus Day, write about the history of tragedies and discoveries at sea!

October 15: Write about the history of the Salem witch trials. What is Wicca? How has it changed through the years?

October 16: If a couple were to have a Halloween themed wedding what would that be like?

October 17: What are some inexpensive ways to decorate and remodel a home – or even just a workspace?

October 18: This is Adopt a Shelter Dog Month! Dogs have long been considered to be man's best friend. A popular quote about dogs is : *If you want someone who never criticizes what you do, doesn't care if you are pretty or ugly, fat or thin, young or old, who acts as if every word you say is especially worthy of listening to, and loves you unconditionally...then adopt a dog.*

Write about a dog that was important to you.

October 19: Write a health piece for adults about colds, stomach "bugs," and the flu – how to tell them apart and ways to treat each one.

October 20: Write about the person who scared/scares you the most?

October 21: The third Saturday of October is Sweetest Day! Write the last sentence from any book and use it as the first sentence in a book/article about love and relationships.

October 22: On October 22, 1983, a Navajo Churro blanket was bought for $115,000 at Sotheby's. A fragment of a hand woven tapestry from the 1430's was sold at an auction for $1,124,794. Most of us had a favorite blanket as a child and even as a teen. Even adults have a favorite blanket. Write about the favorites blankets that you and/or your children have had.

October 23: What are some creative solutions to common household problems?

October 24: Do you believe in ghosts? Why or why not?

October 25: What are the most haunted places in America. Have you been anywhere that was haunted?

October 26: During International Drum Month, write about famous drummers, their lives and their triumphs.

October 27: Write a letter to someone who has passed away.

October 28: Write a biography about someone in history that you greatly admire!

October 29: Write about life in the Middle Ages. What are some of their beliefs?

October 30: For Domestic Violence Awareness Month write an opinion piece about any clashes that you had with domestic violence. What would you teach teens today about domestic violence?

October 31: Write a timeline of Halloween history!

NOVEMBER

November 1: November is known as NaNo WriMo. That stands for National Novel Writing Month. Do you have an idea for a book that you always wanted to write? Now is a great time to do that! Remember, the challenge of NaNo WriMo is to write a book in 30 days!

November 2: Card games got their start in the 9th century. Some card games are no longer played. Magic and Pokeman took card games to a whole new level Write about the history of card games.

November 3: What are the best ways that people can follow an "anger management" regime.

November 4: For King Tut Day, write about the life of King Tut and Cleopatra. To this day, no one knows for certain how King Tut died, though there are several theories, from a broken leg that led to an infected wound – to a bite from a hippopotamus. Which theory would you follow?

November 5: Write an opinion piece about bullies.

November 6: What are 100 things that every teen should do before turning 21 years old.

November 7: Many people are not happy with the direction of our government. What do you think of what our government has become like. Do you think Congress should be fired? Do you think the president should be impeached.

November 8: Write about a time that someone saved your life – physically or mentally!

November 9: Miss Manners was the first newspaper column to talk about proper etiquette. Write an advice piece that teachers all the rules and habits of proper etiquette.

November 10: Mark Twain described forgiveness as "the fragrance that the violet sheds on the heel that has crushed it." Write about the different (and creative) ways to tell someone that you are sorry.

November 11: The Masons are a Secret Society for men. The Red Hat Society is a group for women over the age of 50. The are known by their trademark red hat – with purple ribbon. Write about the history of secret societies groups for adults.

November 12: Today is Chicken Soup for the Soul Day! Write a series of short stories of events that you experienced or witnessed – events that changed your heart for the better.

November 13: Write a consumer awareness piece with tips on shopping smart and avoiding scams. Include couponing craze!

November 14: What would you have for your dream birthday party? What gifts would you want? Who would you want there – if you could invite anyone?

November 15: Write about a friend or family member that you lost touch with. Why did you lose touch? What would you tell them if you were reunited?

November 16: They say that the sense of smell can trigger long-forgotten memories. What are the scents that bring back (good and bad) memories for you?

November 17: Hitchhikers are kidnapped and murdered every year. It does not happen to every hitchhiker but the dangers are just as real. Write about the dangerous situations that you put yourself in, intentionally or not.

November 18: What are some ways that couples can be more romantic and spice up their sex life?

November 19: Write about animals that have saved people's lives.

November 20: In 1899, 68 year old, Henry Bliss, was helping a friend from a street car when he was struck by taxi driver, Jacob German, who was intoxicated. Bliss became the first person killed in an automobile accident, as well as the first person killed by a drunk driver. German became the first person arrested for speeding. At the time there was no such charge as "DUI," since then it was not illegal to drink and drive. Write about the history of the highway system.

November 21: Every year there is a Cat Festival in Belgian. Cat lovers from around the world attend the festival which begins with a "Cat Parade!" Write about cats – the ways we love cats and the history of cats in the world.

November 22: Write a how-to piece on small home improvement jobs.

November 23: Write about the history of diet crazes!

November 24: What are some of the problems that families face today?

November 25: Did you know that the first Thanksgiving was actually 3 days long and they did not eat turkey? When the pilgrims landed on Plymouth Rock they were ill and starving. It was the Wampanoag tribe that saved the pilgrims and taught them to hunt, fish and harvest crops. The first Thanksgiving was a celebration in their first successful harvest, which could not have been accomplished without the Wampanoag tribe. Write a story about the events of those days.

November 26: Make a list of metaphors – as many as you can think of. Now, work on how you can expand on the basic metaphors, like, "skinny as a rail" or "so hungry, I can eat a horse!"

November 27: Celebrate Pins and Needles Day, write about something you were afraid and nervous about doing but mustered up the courage to do it anyway!

November 28: Write a how-to guide about the hobby of scrapbooking.

November 29: Write a comparison article of students lives from the 60's to students today – and students from 100 years ago!

November 30: Write about depression and the battles that people face with it. Have you or someone you know ever suffered from depression? What are some of the ways that people can fight depression?

DECEMBER

December 1: Make a list of activity ideas to celebrate advent.

December 2: What are some easy Christmas or Hanukkah traditions that families can start having now! Make them fun and creative!

December 3: Do you believe in angels? Write about the history and different beliefs of angels.

December 4: Write about everything that you enjoy about winter!

December 5: Write about the first snowfall of the year!

December 6: Make a step-by-step piece on all the ways to build and design a Gingerbread House!

December 7: For Letter Writing Day, write 5 letters – by hand - to friends and/or family. Now mail them!!

December 8: President Benjamin Harrison was the first US President to have a Christmas tree in the White House. Write about the history and the traditions of the Christmas tree.

December 9: This is Christmas Card Day! Make Christmas cards and deliver them to elderly in nursing homes and the elderly in your neighborhood. Include a candy cane and a packet of hot chocolate!

December 10: It is said that it is better to give than to receive. Write 100 inexpensive ways that people can give!

December 11: The eyes are the windows to the soul. Write about body language and how our behavior can reveal hidden thoughts and emotions.

December 12: What are the different ways that countries celebrate Christmas? What are their legendary beliefs about Santa Claus?

December 13: Write about the best gifts to buy for children (age-by-age) and teens.

December 14: Write a Q&A Piece on the 50 states.

December 15: As a Christmas present for your family, create a book of 1,001 Fun Family Facts and make copies as gifts for everyone at the family Christmas party!

December 16: Write an opinion piece about people stand strong for animal rights. Do you agree with their beliefs? Which ones?

December 17: On December 17, 1803, the Wright Brothers flew the first airplane. Write about the history of flight – from the hot air balloon to NASA's rockets.

December 18: Tim McGraw is noted for saying, "We all take different paths in life, but no matter where we go, we take a little of each other everywhere." Write about all of the people that came into your life and shaped you into the person that you are today. Include the good and the bad.

December 19: Make a character journal of names, professions, cities, and other unique characteristics that you may one day use in a story.

December 20: Write the last line from your favorite movie and use it as the first line in a book about Christmas!

December 21: Write 10 Christmas memories – good or bad!

December 22: Write about the 5 people who had the biggest impact in your life – good or bad!

December 23: Write a family biography about someone who adopted a child/children. How was the idea of adoption first suggested? Write about their new family experience from then and now.

December 24: What is the first book you read, that made you want to be a writer.

December 25: Write about a time that you witnessed or experienced a miracle.

December 26: If you were going to write a daily blog what would it be about and why?

December 27: What is your biggest personal triumph?

December 28: Start making your own list of 365 Days of Writing for next year! You don't have to finish it by January 1st, you can build on as the year passes by. Start a blog and share the days and with others!

December 29: Map out a timeline of Christmas books. From the very best that were written over 100 years ago, that are still read today – to new Christmas stories that will become classics for our grandchildren. Don't forget the few in between that have not received the notoriety that they deserve. Now try a few of the other holidays!

December 30: Make a Family Christmas Story. Write the first 2 pages of a winter/Christmas adventure book. Over the next year ahead, contact each family member and have each one write a piece of the book. For example, one of your cousin's write pages 3 & 4, a sibling writes pages 5 & 6, etc. Then you write the last 2 pages. Take your time, give yourself the whole year to complete the book. At Christmas time next year, make a copy of the book for each person that helped contribute!

December 31: Write 50 fun New Year's Eve traditions! Here are your first five:

Have a "Toast to a Change" with your friends and family. During the toast, you each say something that you want to change or do in the upcoming year! Something other than dieting or quitting smoking!

Other titles from Higher Ground Books & Media:

Wise Up to Rise Up by Rebecca Benston

A Path to Shalom by Steen Burke

From a Hole in My Life to a Life Made Whole by Janet Kay Teresa

Overcomer by Forrest Henslee

Miracles: I Love Them by Forest Godin

32 Days with Christ's Passion by Mark Etter

The Magic Egg by Linda Phillipson

The Tin Can Gang by Chuck David

Whobert the Owl by Mya C. Benston

Dear You by Derra Nicole Sabo

A Whale of a Tale by Uncle Dave Howard

Add these titles to your collection today!

www.ingramcontent.com/pod-product-compliance
Lightning Source LLC
Chambersburg PA
CBHW022134280326
41933CB00007B/693